East South-Central States

Kentucky
Tennessee

Tish Davidson

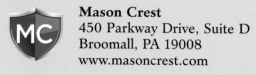

Mason Crest
450 Parkway Drive, Suite D
Broomall, PA 19008
www.masoncrest.com

©2016 by Mason Crest, an imprint of National Highlights, Inc.

Printed and bound in the United States of America.

CPSIA Compliance Information: Batch #LES2015.
For further information, contact Mason Crest at 1-866-MCP-Book.

First printing
1 3 5 7 9 8 6 4 2

Library of Congress Cataloging-in-Publication Data

Davidson, Tish.
    East south-central states : Kentucky and Tennessee / Tish Davidson.
        pages cm. — (Let's explore the states)
    Includes bibliographical references and index.
    ISBN 978-1-4222-3322-1 (hc)
    ISBN 978-1-4222-8607-4 (ebook)
    1. Southern States—Juvenile literature. 2. Kentucky—Juvenile literature.
    3. Tennessee—Juvenile literature. I. Title.
    F209.3.D38 2016
    976.8—dc23

                                2015008421

Let's Explore the States series ISBN: 978-1-4222-3319-1

About the Author: Tish Davidson has written many articles for newspapers and magazines. Her books for middle school readers include *African American Scientists and Inventors, Theocracy,* and *Facing Competition.* Davidson lives in Fremont, California, and is a volunteer puppy raiser for Guide Dogs for the Blind.

Picture Credits: Architect of the Capitol: 18; Senator Lamar Alexander: 51; Everett Historical: 21 (bottom), 22 (top), 28 (top), 49 (bottom); The Hermitage: Home of President Andrew Jackson, Nashville, TN: 44 (top); Library of Congress: 17, 21 (top), 22 (bottom), 46, 49 (top), 55; Photos.com: 14; used under license from Shutterstock, Inc.: 1, 5 (bottom), 6, 7, 10, 11, 12, 15, 24, 29, 30 (top), 34, 35, 36, 37, 38, 39, 41, 43, 50, 53, 56, 59; Aceshot1 / Shutterstock.com: 57; Natalia Bratslavsky / Shutterstock.com: 58 (top); S. Bukley / Shutterstock.com: 28; Christopher Halloran / Shutterstock.com: 25; Jessica Kirsh / Shutterstock.com: 26; James R. Martin / Shutterstock.com: 52; Irina Mos / Shutterstock.com: 27, 31; Joseph Sohm / Shutterstock.com: 5 (top), 58 (bottom), 60; University of Kentucky Athletic Department: 30 (bottom); The Woolaroc Museum: 44 (bottom).

Table of Contents

KEY ICONS TO LOOK FOR:

Words to Understand: These words with their easy-to-understand definitions will increase the reader's understanding of the text, while building vocabulary skills.

Sidebars: This boxed material within the main text allows readers to build knowledge, gain insights, explore possibilities, and broaden their perspectives by weaving together additional information to provide realistic and holistic perspectives.

Research Projects: Readers are pointed toward areas of further inquiry connected to each chapter. Suggestions are provided for projects that encourage deeper research and analysis.

Text-Dependent Questions: These questions send the reader back to the text for more careful attention to the evidence presented there.

Series Glossary of Key Terms: This back-of-the book glossary contains terminology used throughout this series. Words found here increase the reader's ability to read and comprehend higher-level books and articles in this field.

LET'S EXPLORE THE STATES

Atlantic: North Carolina, Virginia, West Virginia
Central Mississippi River Basin: Arkansas, Iowa, Missouri
East South-Central States: Kentucky, Tennessee
Eastern Great Lakes: Indiana, Michigan, Ohio
Gulf States: Alabama, Louisiana, Mississippi
Lower Atlantic: Florida, Georgia, South Carolina
Lower Plains: Kansas, Nebraska
Mid-Atlantic: Delaware, District of Columbia, Maryland
Non-Continental: Alaska, Hawaii
Northern New England: Maine, New Hampshire, Vermont
Northeast: New Jersey, New York, Pennsylvania
Northwest: Idaho, Oregon, Washington
Rocky Mountain: Colorado, Utah, Wyoming
Southern New England: Connecticut, Massachusetts, Rhode Island
Southwest: New Mexico, Oklahoma, Texas
U.S. Territories and Possessions
Upper Plains: Montana, North Dakota, South Dakota
The West: Arizona, California, Nevada
Western Great Lakes: Illinois, Minnesota, Wisconsin

ILLINOIS

INDIANA

OHIO

Maysville

Ashland

Louisville   Frankfort

Lexington

WEST
VIRGINIA

Henderson   Owensboro

Bardstown

Richmond

Paintsville

KENTUCKY

Elizabethtown   Danville

Pikeville

Campbellsville

Cairo   Paducah

MISSOURI

Bowling Green

Somerset

Hazard

Glasgow

Harlan

Hopkinsville

Middlesboro

VIRGINIA

Mississippi River

Ohio River

MAMMOTH CAVE
NATIONAL PARK

TENNESSEE

Kentucky at a Glance

Area: 40,411 sq mi (104,644 sq km)[1].
(37th largest state.)
Land: 39,732 sq mi (102,906 sq km)
Water: 679 sq miles (1,759 sq km)
Highest elevation: Black Mountain,
4,145 feet (1,263 m)
Lowest elevation: Mississippi River,
257 feet (78 m)

Statehood: June 1, 1792 (15th state)
Capital: Frankfort

Population: 4,413,457
(26th largest state)[2]

State nickname: Bluegrass State
State bird: Cardinal
State flower: Goldenrod

[1] *U.S. Census Bureau*
[2] *U.S. Census Bureau, 2014 estimate*

Kentucky

Kentucky was once considered the Far West. Early pioneers discovered a rough, forested land full of wild animals and unpredictable Native Americans. Settlers had to grow their own food, make their own tools, and settle their own disputes. They valued hard work and independence. When the Civil War came, each Kentuckian felt free to make up his or her own mind about whether to support the North or the South. Families were torn apart by differing loyalties.

Today Kentucky is no longer wild, isolated, or divided. Roads crisscross the state bringing tourists to enjoy the beauty of the Cumberland Mountains and admire the horse farms of the Bluegrass Region. Coal mined in the state and goods made in Kentucky factories are shipped around the world. Buyers from many countries come to the state to buy *Thoroughbred* racehorses. But the citizens of Kentucky still put a high value on independence, self-reliance, and the right to make their own decisions.

Words to Understand in This Chapter

abolitionist—a person who wanted to abolish, or get rid of, slavery.

alliance—a formal agreement between two governments to support each other.

auditor—an unbiased person who examines the financial health of an organization.

artifact—an object such as a tool, weapon, or pottery made by people in the past.

Commonwealth—meaning "for the common good," in the United States it is the same as a state. Massachusetts, Pennsylvania, Virginia, and Kentucky all identify themselves as commonwealths.

electoral votes—Although the people vote in a popular election for the president, the president is officially elected by electoral votes. Each state has the number of votes equal to the total of its US senators and representatives.

median—middle.

neutral—not supporting one side of a disagreement or the other.

nursery plants—plants usually started in greenhouses and sold to landscapers and gardeners.

pelts—animal skins with the fur still attached.

poverty level—the level of income below which a person or family is declared poor by government standards.

secede—to withdraw; specifically for a state to leave the United States.

segregated—separated by race.

Thoroughbred—a breed of horses mainly used for racing that can trace their heritage back to horses developed in England in the 1600s.

veto—a decision by an individual in power not to allow something such as a governor not allowing a measure passed by the legislature to become law.

yearling—a Thoroughbred racehorse that is one year old.

Geography

Kentucky is an inland state in the east-central United States. The state is about 380 miles (610 km) long and 140 miles (225 km) wide. Kentucky shares a border with seven other states. The eastern side touches the tip of Virginia and is separated from West Virginia by the Big Sandy and Tug Fork rivers. The northern border with Ohio, Indiana, and Illinois is formed by the Ohio River. The Mississippi River separates Kentucky from Missouri on the southwest. On the south, the state shares a long, straight border with Tennessee. The eastern part of Kentucky is in the Eastern Time Zone. The western part is in the Central Time Zone.

Kentucky contains five land regions. The Cumberland Plateau is the easternmost region. The land is mountainous, with high, flat land (plateaus) separated by deep valleys. Black Mountain, the highest point in the state, is in this region. The Cumberland Plateau also contains the Eastern Kentucky Coal Field. The Cumberland Gap is at the southeast

 Did You Know?

What's so special about Kentucky bluegrass? To start with, the grass isn't blue. The leaves are green, but if the grass is allowed to grow tall, it sends up seed stalks that have bluish color. The soil in the Bluegrass Region contains a lot of calcium. As bluegrass grows, it absorbs some of this calcium. Horses grazing on Kentucky bluegrass use that calcium to build strong, healthy bones. This gives them an advantage over horses raised in other areas. Bluegrass has helped make Lexington the Horse Capital of the World.

corner of the Plateau. Thousands of pioneers used this break in the mountains to reach the West.

The Bluegrass Region in the north central part of the state is the most heavily populated region. The Inner Bluegrass has rolling fields and rich farmland. This area is known for its Thoroughbred horse farms. The Outer Bluegrass is a hillier region that surrounds the Inner Bluegrass. Beyond the Outer Bluegrass is a narrow band

The Bluegrass region, with its rolling hills, is ideal for horse farms.

Stalactites and stalagmites in Mammoth Cave, one of the world's largest known cave systems. The entrance is located in southwestern Kentucky.

called The Knobs. It is named for hundreds of separate, cone-shaped hills found in the area.

The Pennyroyal Plateau spreads across most of the state's southern border. Its name comes from an herb that grows there. This region is famous for its limestone caves. Mammoth Cave, the longest cave system in the world, has tunnels that stretch for about 400 miles (644 km) under the region.

Northwest of the Pennyroyal Plateau lies the Western Coal Field.

A coal processing facility in the Western Coal Field region of Kentucky.

Coal is mined in this rocky, hilly region. The Ohio River forms the western border of the coalfields. A small strip of good farmland lies along the river. The Jackson Purchase is in southwestern Kentucky. It is surrounded by three rivers: the Ohio on the north, the Mississippi on the west, and the Tennessee River on the east. This flat, swampy area is named for Andrew Jackson, who later became president of the United States. He bought this land and part of what is now Tennessee from the Chickasaw tribe in 1818.

Fall leaves bring bright colors to this Cumberland River valley in southeastern Kentucky.

Kentucky has a four-season climate with warm, humid summers and cool winters. Summer highs average around 87°F (31°C) and winter lows average around 23°F (–5°C). Average precipitation is 46 inches (120 cm) per year. The southern part of the state gets more rain than the northern part. In the winter, snow falls in the mountains. The coldest temperature, –37°F (–38°C), was recorded in 1994.

Violent weather is common in Kentucky. Ice and snowstorms can occur in winter. Tornadoes often rip across the state in spring, and flooding of the state's rivers is a common occurrence. Heat waves often bake the state in summer. The highest recorded temperature was 114 °F (46 °C) in 1930.

History

The area that is now Kentucky was inhabited long before European settlers arrived. Around 1000 BCE, a group of people called the Adena settled in the Ohio Valley. What we know about them comes from the *artifacts* found in large mounds where they buried important people, tools, and objects their society valued. Several hundred of these mounds are found in the state. The mound building culture disappeared around 1300 CE. Some of the best-preserved mounds are at Wickliffe Mounds State Historic Site in western Kentucky.

The first Europeans to see Kentucky were French fur traders who explored the Ohio and Mississippi Rivers. They passed through the area, but did not stay. Native Americans did not build permanent settlements in Kentucky either, but many tribes claimed Kentucky as their hunting grounds and visited regularly. The Shawnee in the north and west, the Cherokee in the southeast, and the Chickasaw in the southwest tip of the state were the Native tribes that most strongly resisted European settlement. As of 2014, the Southern Cherokee Nation of Kentucky and the Ridgetop Shawnee are the only tribes recognized by the state.

Kentucky was originally was part of Virginia Colony, but because the mountains of the Cumberland Plateau

Daniel Boone leads settlers through the Cumberland Gap into Kentucky. This route through the mountains enabled Europeans to explore and settle the lands known as Kentucky and Tennessee.

were difficult to cross, little was known about the area. In 1750, The Loyal Land Company of Virginia sent Thomas Walker and five other men into what is now Kentucky. These explorers were looking for good farmland for the company to buy. The men traveled for four months but never reached the Bluegrass Region and the good land they were seeking. Today, Thomas Walker is remembered for naming the Cumberland Gap.

The Cumberland Gap is a break in the mountains. It had been used by Native Americans for years, but Walker's writings about his exploration of Kentucky made it known to Europeans. The Gap became a gateway to the West. Between 1775 and 1810, 200,000 to 300,000 people used the Gap as the easiest route through the mountains. Today it is part of the Cumberland Gap National Historic Park.

Kentucky was a wild place. Bison grazed on the grasslands. Bears and wolves roamed the forests, and fur-bearing animals were abundant. During the 1760s, small groups of men traveled into the mountains to hunt these animals. The hunters were called "long hunters" because their hunts could last up to two years. Long hunting was risky. Sometimes hunters were captured or killed by Native Americans or were robbed of a year's worth of *pelts*. But for some long hunters, the unsettled land offered irresistible opportunities.

Daniel Boone was the best known of the long hunters. He traveled in Kentucky several times beginning in 1767. In 1775, Boone was hired by the Transylvania Land Company to lead a group of thirty-two people to cut a road from the Cumberland Gap to the Ohio River near present-day Louisville. This became known as the Wilderness Road. Along the way, Boone established Fort Boonesborough on the Kentucky River. Today the fort is part of Boonesborough State Park. It has been rebuilt to look like it did during Boone's lifetime.

At the time of the American Revolution (1775–1783), Kentucky was a county of Virginia, but when war broke out, Virginia did not send supplies to help Kentuckians defend themselves. Native American tribes

The candle making shop at Fort Boonesborough, which is now a state park.

were already attacking European settlers for building homes and hunting on their land. The British encouraged these attacks. The settlers had few choices. They could move into forts at Boonesborough and Harrodsburg, return to more populated and better defended parts of Virginia, or risk being captured or killed. At one point, during the War, Kentucky had a population of only about 300 settlers.

Following American independence, Kentucky became attractive to people looking for good, cheap land. Settlers arrived by two routes. People from Virginia and states in the southeast came through the Cumberland Gap and followed the Wilderness Road. Many of these settlers brought slaves with them. People from Pennsylvania, Maryland, and West Virginia, floated down the Ohio River on flat-bottomed boats and often settled along the river. By 1790, about 73,000 people lived in Kentucky County.

Kentucky County had little in common with the eastern part of Virginia. As early as 1782, some leaders in Kentucky began working toward making the region a separate state. The Virginia legislature agreed to this idea, but it took almost ten years to work out the details. Some Kentuckians wanted to leave the United States completely and form an *alliance* with Spain. At that time, Spain controlled a large amount of land west of the Mississippi River. Other Kentuckians were concerned about keeping their land and property rights, including their slaves, which were considered property. The Virginia government wanted Kentucky to take a share of Virginia's debt from the Revolutionary War, and the federal government wanted to make sure the Ohio River could be used freely by people from all states. Eventually, compromises were worked out, and on June 1, 1792, Kentucky became the fifteenth state. It entered the Union as a slave state.

Kentucky sent about 25,700 men into battle during the War of 1812 (1812–1814). This war was fought against Great Britain. The men recruited from Kentucky were to march through Ohio to Detroit and invade Canada, but the plan failed. At the end of the war, Kentucky soldiers were also involved in the Battle of New Orleans. This battle, won by the Americans, was fought after the war had officially ended because neither side had gotten the news that the war was over. More than half of the soldiers that died in the War of 1812 were from Kentucky.

Most of the settlers that came to Kentucky in the early 1800s were farmers who moved to the Bluegrass Region. At first, they grew corn and wheat and raised hogs and chickens to feed their families. Later they grew tobacco and hemp, a plant whose fibers were used to make rope and clothing. These products were often shipped from port cities such as Louisville down the Ohio River to the Mississippi River and then on to New Orleans. Growing hemp and tobacco required a lot of labor, much of it done by slaves. By 1830, Kentucky had a population of about 518,000 white people, 165,000 slaves, and 4,900 free black people.

Slaves had lived in Kentucky from the time it was part of Virginia Colony. However, many Kentuckians thought slavery was wrong. In 1792 when

A Kentucky militia led by Colonel Richard M. Johnson participated in a major American victory of the War of 1812. In October 1813, an American army led by William Henry Harrison defeated a British force of about 600 soldiers and about 1,000 of their Shawnee Native American allies at the Battle of the Thames in Ontario, Canada. Johnson was credited with killing the Native American leader Tecumseh, as this nineteenth century illustration shows.

Kentucky became a state, a minister named David Rice pushed the legislature to include language in Kentucky's constitution that would prevent people from bringing more slaves into the state and would gradually free slaves already there. His attempt failed by a vote of 26 to 16, and slavery remained legal.

Many Kentuckians were still opposed to slavery. In the 1830s, Cassius Marcellus Clay, the *abolitionist* son of a wealthy slaveholder, published an anti-slavery newspaper in Lexington. Clay's life was threatened and his property attacked because of his belief that slavery was wrong. Eventually, he moved to Ohio, a free state, where he continued to publish and speak about ending slavery.

Ending slavery was a national issue. Tension between North and South boiled over. The Civil War (1861–1865) began when states in the Deep South *seceded* from the United States to form the Confederate States

Senator Henry Clay of Kentucky was one of the most powerful national leaders during the first half of the nineteenth century. Here, he presents legislation to the U.S. Senate in 1850 intended to prevent civil war from occurring. The Compromise of 1850 did prevent the sectional conflict for a decade, but ultimately the northern and southern states split after Abraham Lincoln was elected president in 1860.

of America (CSA). Kentucky was caught in the middle. Settlers who had arrived by traveling down the Ohio River from the North generally opposed slavery and wanted to stay in the Union. Settlers who came from the South through the Cumberland Gap generally supported slavery. They wanted Kentucky to join the Confederacy.

Individual Kentuckians chose whether to support the North or the South. Families were torn apart. The government of Kentucky responded by declaring the state *neutral*. Unfortunately, neutrality did not keep Kentucky from being pulled into the war. The state was too important to both sides because of the men, horses, and food it could supply. Both the Union and the Confederacy sent troops into Kentucky. Eventually about 35,000 men fought for the South and 75,000 men, including 28,000 freed slaves, fought for the North.

Kentucky recovered slowly from the Civil War. Most people still lived on small farms. Tobacco replaced

 Did You Know?

The vault at Fort Knox, between Louisville and Elizabethtown, is where the United States Treasury Department has stored the gold reserves of the United States since 1937. In 2014, 147.3 million ounces (4.176 million kg) of gold were in the vault. The gold is in bars weighing about 27.5 pounds (12.3 kg). In the past, other valuable items such as the original Declaration of Independence and Lincoln's Gettysburg Address have been stored here too.

hemp as the main crop grown for cash. Even before the war, Kentuckians had made liquor by distilling corn and other grains. After the war, manufacturing whiskey became a major industry. Coal mining also expanded. Kentucky went from producing 150,000 tons of coal in 1870 to 5.3 million tons in 1900 to 60.7 million tons in 1929.

New railroad lines and better roads brought European immigrants into the state. Between 1870 and 1900, the population of Kentucky grew by about 826,000 people. At the same time, many former slaves left the state for better opportunities in northern cities such as Chicago, Detroit, and New York.

The twentieth century started with a bang on January 31, 1900, when William Goebel was shot. Goebel had just been declared the winner of a violently disputed election for governor. He died one hundred hours later. His death set off fistfights, feuds, and a political crisis that lasted for months.

A few years later in 1904, the Black Patch War broke out over tobacco. Almost all tobacco raised in Kentucky was bought by three companies. These companies agreed among themselves to pay farmers very low prices. The prices they offered were less than it cost to grow the crop. The farmers united and refused to sell their tobacco. Not all farmers agreed with this plan. Some went ahead and sold their crop. They were threatened, beaten up, and had their homes and fields burned by a group known as the Night Riders. The violence lasted four years until tobacco prices rose.

World War I (1914–1918) increased the demand for coal, food, and supplies for the troops. Between 1914 and 1920, Kentucky almost doubled its coal production. Kentucky also contributed men to the war effort. About 84,000 Kentuckians fought in World War I.

Coal mining was a dirty, dangerous job. After the war, between 1920 and 1929, more than 1,600 people died in mine accidents in Kentucky. Violence occurred at many mines when miner owners tried to stop miners from joining unions. The miners wanted to organize so they could demand better pay and safer working conditions. Then in 1929, the stock market crashed and the Great Depression began. Demand for coal dropped. Mines shut down. Many miners lived in company towns where their homes were owned by the coal company. When they lost their jobs, they and their families became homeless. At that time, there were no government programs to help them.

Coal sits in chutes near a mine in Knox County. Since the nineteenth century coal has been an important resource of the state.

Class is in session at this school for African-American children in Anthoston, 1916. Half of the students are missing from the class because they were in the fields picking tobacco.

A coal miner hangs his check tag onto a board, signifying that he is safely out of the mine at the end of his work shift. The chalked note below indicates that the mine is closing. During the 1930s, the economic downturn known as the Great Depression hit Kentucky families hard.

Kentucky farmers gather to watch a mule being traded near the Works Progress Administration office in Wolfe County, 1940. The Works Progress Administration was a federal government program that was intended to help put Americans back to work during the Great Depression. It was part of Franklin D. Roosevelt's New Deal package of programs.

The Depression was so severe, that by 1934, new federal government programs were in place to help people who were out of work. The Civilian Conservation Corps planted trees and built trails in Kentucky's parks. The Tennessee Valley Authority built dams that provided construction jobs, and the Rural Electrification Administration brought electricity to isolated areas.

More factory jobs became available after World War II (1941–1945) began, but factories in the North paid better wages than factories in Kentucky. Many people left the state in search of higher pay. In addition, almost 307,000 Kentuckians served in the armed forces during the war.

When World War II ended, Kentucky was still a *segregated* state. Black and white children did not go to school together. Black and white adults could not eat at the same restaurants. However, the University of Kentucky began accepting African American students in 1948. So when the U. S. Supreme Court ruled in 1954 that racially segregated schools were illegal, integration of the school system proceeded slowly, but without the violence that occurred in many southern states. In 1966, Kentucky passed the strongest civil rights law in the South, and by 1967, most public places were desegregated.

The 1970s brought the challenge of protecting Kentucky's environment. Surface mining scrapes coal from the top layers of the earth, rather than digging it out using underground tunnels. Years of surface mining had left acres of treeless land. With no trees to hold the soil in place, dirt washed off hillsides and polluted the rivers. In 1977, Kentucky passed laws to protect the environment by limiting surface mining.

In the late 1980s, Kentucky began to improve its public education system. First, it made changes in how schools were funded. This made more money available for education and distributed the money more equally. Kentucky also developed new academic standards to better prepare students for successful careers.

A better-prepared workforce attracted new businesses. In 2006,

Toyota began manufacturing the Camry in Georgetown, Kentucky. Other manufacturers followed. However, like the rest of the country, Kentucky experienced an economic slowdown beginning around 2008, with recovery still slow in 2014. Going forward in the twenty-first century, Kentucky will face challenges to the environment, education, health care, and job creation.

Government

The *Commonwealth* of Kentucky is governed from its capital, Frankfort, under its fourth state constitution written in 1891. The constitution divides state government into executive, legislative, and judicial branches.

The executive branch is headed by the governor. The governor prepares the state budget and signs (approves) or *vetoes* laws passed by the legislative branch. The lieutenant governor takes over if the governor is unable to perform his or her duties. The governor and the lieutenant governor are elected every four years. Other elected officials in the executive branch are the attorney general, secretary of state, treasur-

The Kentucky State Capitol building has been the seat of the state government since 1910. The building houses offices and chambers for all three branches of the state government.

er, and the **auditor** of public accounts.

The legislative branch is called the General Assembly. It has two divisions, the Senate, with 38 members, and the House of Representatives with 100 members. The legislature is responsible for proposing and passing laws. Representatives are elected every two years. Senators are elected every four years.

The judicial branch enforces the laws. Minor cases (misdemeanors) are heard in district courts. More serious cases (felonies) are heard in circuit courts. Decisions from these courts can be taken to the Court of Appeals for review and finally to the Supreme Court. The Supreme Court has seven members who are elected for eight-year terms. The Supreme Court reviews all death penalty cases and other serious cases, and can declare that a law passed by the legislature violates the state constitution.

Kentucky sends two Senators and six Representatives to Washington D.C. to represent them in Congress. This gives the state eight **electoral votes** in presidential elections.

Rand Paul has represented Kentucky in the U.S. Senate since 2011. In 2015 he launched a campaign for president of the United States.

The Economy

From the time Kentucky was settled until the 1950s, it was an agricultural state. Today Kentucky has about 77,000 farms, most of which are small family farms. In 2012, Kentucky produced more tobacco than any other state. Kentucky farmers also grow large amounts of corn, hay, soybeans, and wheat. More than 33,000 farms raise beef cattle.

Horses are a billion dollar industry in Kentucky. The state has 35,000 horse farms, most located in the

The Kentucky Derby, held each May at Churchill Downs racetrack in Louisville, is one of the most prestigious events in American horse racing.

Bluegrass Region. Thoroughbred racehorses from Kentucky are sold to buyers throughout the world. In addition, horseracing and horse tourism bring 800,000 visitors to the Kentucky Horse Park outside Lexington each year and many more to racecourses such as Churchill Downs, home of the Kentucky Derby.

Coal has been mined in Kentucky for more than 200 years. However, the demand for clean energy has reduced the use of coal. In 2013, the state produced 80.5 million tons of coal, the lowest amount since 1963.

Beginning in the 1950s, manufacturing grew in importance in the state. Toyota, Ford, and General Motors all build automobiles in Kentucky. Other factories make trailers, railroad cars, parts for jet engines, and home appliances such as washing machines. The famous Louisville Slugger baseball bat has been made in Louisville since 1884. Although manufacturing is important to the state, in 2014, most Kentuckians work in service industries such as retail stores, restaurants, hospitals, education, and government services.

People in Kentucky earn less than the national average income. Between 2008 and 2012, the *median* household income in Kentucky was $42,610, almost $11,000 less than the national average. However, Kentucky is one of the least expensive states to live in, and a higher percentage of people own their homes in Kentucky (68.7 percent) than the national average (65.5 percent). Still, 18.6 percent of resi-

dents have incomes that fall below the *poverty* level.

The People

In the census of 1800, Kentucky had 73,077 residents of which 11,944 (about 16.4 percent) were African American, almost all of whom were slaves. By 2013, the population had grown to about 4,395,300. Only 2.3 percent of the population was born in

Kentucky is known for a type of whiskey known as bourbon. The state is home to several producers of this alcoholic spirit, including the Wild Turkey distillery in Lawrenceburg.

Famous People from Kentucky

Kentucky was the birthplace of two presidents on opposite sides during the Civil War. Abraham Lincoln (1809–1865), sixteenth president of the United States, was born in a cabin in Hardin County. His family later moved to Illinois. Jefferson Davis (1808–1889), president of the Confederate States of America, was born on a farm in Christian County, but grew up on a cotton plantation in Mississippi.

Abraham Lincoln   Jefferson Davis

Bluegrass music grew out of music played in the Kentucky mountains. Bill Monroe (1911–1996) popularized bluegrass in the 1940s. Today dozens of bluegrass music festivals are held in Kentucky each year. Present-day country music stars that were born in Kentucky include Naomi Judd (b. 1946) and her daughter Wynonna (b. 1964), both born in Ashland. Billy Ray Cyrus (b. 1961) is from Lexington, and Loretta Lynn (b. 1935) was born in Butcher Hollow. Lynn's life story was made into the movie *Coal Miner's Daughter* in 1980.

Loretta Lynn

Television journalist Diane Sawyer (b. 1945) was born in Glasgow and got her start in television at a Louisville station. Actors George Clooney (b. 1961) and Jennifer Lawrence (b. 1990) were born in Lexington, while Johnny Depp (b. 1963) is from Owensboro.

Muhammad Ali (b. 1942) is perhaps the most famous athlete to come from the state. Ali was born Cassius Clay in Louisville, but changed his name when he converted to Islam. He won a gold medal in boxing in the 1960 Olympics, was one of the greatest world heavyweight champions of boxing, and was recognized with the Presidential Medal of Freedom. Basketball player Rajon Rondo (b. 1986) grew up in Louisville and played at the University of Kentucky before entering the NBA, where he has made four All-Star teams.

a foreign country, and only 4.8 percent speak a language other than English at home. These percentages are much lower than for the nation as a whole, where 12.9 percent of the population is foreign born and 20.5 percent do not speak English at home.

Kentucky, along with its neighbor West Virginia, is in one of the least racially diverse regions of the country. In 2013, 88.5 percent of the population self-identified as white. This included 3.3 percent who also identified as Hispanic or Latino. In the nation as a whole, Hispanic/Latinos make up about 17 percent of the population. Only 8.2 percent of Kentuckians self-identified as black or African American compared to the 13.2 percent this group contributes to the population the nation. About 3.3 percent of Kentuckians self-identified

The Ohio River flows past Louisville, Kentucky's largest city.

Lexington is Kentucky's second-largest city. It still has a rural feel, thanks to local laws that prevent the area's famous horse farms from being developed into housing or commercial businesses.

The University of Kentucky's basketball team has won over 2,100 games, more than any other college basketball program. The team plays in 23,000-seat Rupp Arena in Lexington. The Wildcats have won eight national championships, most recently in 2012.

either with other races or with more than one race.

In 2013, more Kentucky residents (52 percent) said that they regularly practiced a religion than people in the nation as a whole (48 percent). Of those who practiced religion, almost all were Christians, with Southern Baptists the largest denomination (31 percent). Roman Catholics made up 8 percent of religiously active individuals, while less than 0.5 percent belonged to non-Christian religions.

Compared to the rest of the country, Kentuckians graduate from high school at a slightly lower rate (82.4 percent) than the national average (85.7 percent), and earn four-year college degrees at a much lower rate (21 percent vs. 28.5 percent).

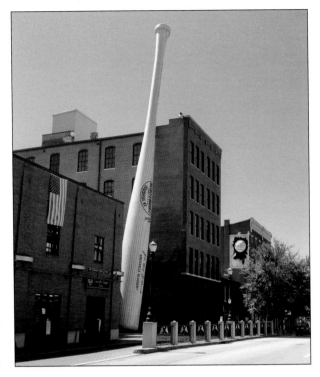

A giant bat stands front of the Louisville Slugger Museum and Factory in downtown Louisville.

Major Cities

Louisville is the state's largest city. Located on the Ohio River, it has a long history as a port. Churchill Downs, the racetrack that has hosted the Kentucky every year since 1875 is located in Louisville. The Kentucky Derby Festival has become a citywide celebration with parties, fireworks, parades, steamboat races, and a hot air balloon festival that starts two weeks before Derby day.

Lexington is called the Horse Capital of the World. The city is home to Keeneland Racetrack. Every year in September, the track hosts a *yearling* auction where buyers from around the world bid millions of dollars on young horses they hope will become the next Kentucky Derby winner. The University of Kentucky is also in Lexington.

Bowling Green in the southwest part of the state is the closest large city to Mammoth Cave National Park and is home to the National Corvette Museum. Every Corvette built in the United States since 1981 was made in Bowling Green, the state's third most populous city.

Smaller towns of interest in Kentucky include *Harrodsburg*, the first permanent settlement in the state; *Hodgenville*, near the birthplace of President Abraham Lincoln; and *Fairview*, birthplace of Jefferson Davis, president of the Confederate States of America during the Civil War.

Further Reading

Davis, Michael D. *Coal Mining Equipment at Work: Featuring the World Famous Mines and Mining Companies of Western Kentucky*. Hudson, Wis.: Iconografixz, 2011.

Gaines, Ann Graham, and William McGevran. *It's My State: Kentucky*. New York: Cavendish Square, 2014.

Hamilton, S. L. *Kentucky Derby*. Edina, Minn.: Abdo Publishing, 2013.

Myers, Marshall. *Only in Old Kentucky: Historic True Tales*. Charleston, SC: The History Press, 2014.

Zronik, John Paul. *Daniel Boone: Woodsman of Kentucky*. New York: Crabtree Publishing, 2006.

Research Project

Surface mining is common in the Eastern Kentucky Coal Field. Do some research on surface mining and write a few paragraphs that describe how it is done and how it changes the environment.

Internet Resources

http://www.americanheritage.com/content/kentucky

The American Heritage Travel Guide to Historic Sites in Kentucky lists historic sites by category with links to each site's webpage.

http://explorekyhistory.ky.gov

Explore Kentucky History provides more than 450 stories about people and places in Kentucky.

http://kentucky.gov

The official state government page provides information about living and working in Kentucky.

http://www.kentuckytourism.com

The official tourism site for the state of Kentucky features events, activities, and places of interest to visitors.

http://kdl.kyvl.org

Hundreds of books, newspapers, maps, and images of Kentucky are available online at the Kentucky Virtual Library.

http://www.nps.gov/maca/index.htm

The National Park Service provides information on the history of Mammoth Cave and on planning a visit.

 # Text-Dependent Questions

1. What is the Wilderness Road?
2. Settlers came into Kentucky by two main routes. What were these routes and who used them?
3. Kentucky was called a border state in the Civil War. What did this mean for Kentucky's participation in the war?

Tennessee at a Glance

Area: 42,143 sq mi (109,150 sq km).[1]
(36th largest state).
Land: 41,217 sq mi (106,752 sq km)
Water: 926 sq mi (2,398 sq km)
Highest elevation: Clingmans Dome,
6,643 feet (2,025 m)
Lowest elevation: Mississippi River,
178 feet (54 m)

Statehood: June 1, 1796 (16th state)
Capital: Nashville

Population: 6,549,352
(16th largest state)[2]

State nickname: the Volunteer State
State bird: mockingbird
State flower: iris

[1] *U.S. Census Bureau*
[2] *U.S. Census Bureau, 2014 estimate*

Tennessee

Tennessee is divided by geography and culture into thirds. People in East Tennessee live in the mountains surrounding Knoxville. They grow tobacco, mine coal, and are known for their bluegrass music, handcrafted quilts, and furniture. The capital, Nashville, dominates Middle Tennessee. Nashville is the home of country music and world-famous universities. Farmers in Middle Tennessee raise beef cattle and hay. Memphis, birthplace of the blues and rock and roll, is the main city in West Tennessee. Cotton and soybeans are raised along the Mississippi River. Together, these three sections make up the thriving state of Tennessee.

Geography

Tennessee is an inland state in the southeastern United States. It measures about 440 (710 km) long and 120 miles (195 km) wide and is roughly the shape of a parallelogram. The state is bordered by eight other states. Kentucky and the southwest tip of Virginia form its border on the north. North Carolina

A fall afternoon in Tennessee farm country.

western two-thirds is in the Central Time Zone.

Tennessee is made up of six land regions. East Tennessee, which begins on the border with North Carolina, is part of the Blue Ridge region. This is an area of 5,000-foot (1,500 m) mountains, many of which lie in Great Smoky Mountains National Park. Clingmans Dome, the highest point in the state, is in the park.

The Appalachian Ridge and Valley region stretches about 55 miles (89 km) west of the Blue Ridge. This is an area of long valleys separated by forest-covered ridges. The cities of Knoxville and Chattanooga are in this region.

The Cumberland Plateau is to the west of the Ridge and Valley region.

is to the east. A long straight southern border separates Tennessee from Georgia, Alabama, and Mississippi. On the west, the Mississippi River forms the border with Arkansas and Missouri. The eastern third of the state is in the Eastern Time Zone. The

Words to Understand in This Chapter

comptroller—an official who supervises financial transactions and financial accounts.

confiscate—to take away private property for public or government use, usually without payment.

Here flat-topped mountains (plateaus) are separated by deep valleys. The Cumberland Plateau is part of the Appalachian Plateau that runs from New York to Alabama.

Beyond the Cumberland Plateau, the Highland Rim surrounds the Nashville Basin. Tobacco grows well in the Highland Rim. Land in the Nashville Basin is also good for farming. Nashville, the capital, is the largest city in Middle Tennessee.

The Gulf Coastal Plain is the westernmost land region. It lies between the Tennessee River and the Mississippi River. It is part of a land region that extends from the Gulf of Mexico to Illinois. This low, swampy

Autumn foliage at Newfound Gap in the Smoky Mountains National Park. This mountain range is located along the border with North Carolina.

View of the Tennessee River as it flows past Chattanooga. The Tennessee River is the largest tributary of the Ohio River, running 652 miles (1,049 km) through the state.

View from Cumberland Gap of Fern Lake. Three states—Kentucky, Tennessee, and Virginia—meet on the ridge in the foreground.

land of West Tennessee floods easily. The region sometimes is called the Delta or the Tennessee Bottoms. Memphis is the main Tennessee city in the Gulf Coastal Plain.

Much of Tennessee has a subtropical climate with hot, humid summers averaging around 90 °F (32 °C) and cool, damp winters. East Tennessee is the coolest region. The average temperature increases as one moves from east to west in the state. On average, 50 inches (130 cm) of precipitation fall on Tennessee each year. Snow falls in the mountains of the Blue Ridge in winter. Crippling ice storms can occur in the winter and in 2011, spring tornadoes killed thirty people.

History

The first people to live in what is now Tennessee arrived about 12,000 years

Mountains along the shore of Watauga Lake, in Cherokee National Forest.

ago. Little is known about where these people came from or why they disappeared. One group, the Mound Builders, lived in Tennessee until about 1300. They built large flat-topped mounds and used them for religious purposes and to bury important people. This culture disappeared before Europeans arrived, but one of their mounds, called Mound Bottom, can be seen at Harpeth River State Park.

By the time Europeans arrived, the land was inhabited by Cherokee, Chickasaw, Creek, and Shawnee tribes. The Cherokee, the largest tribe, lived in East Tennessee. The other large group, the Chickasaw, controlled West Tennessee. The Creek lived in the southern part of Middle Tennessee, and the Shawnee moved into northern Middle Tennessee from Kentucky.

In 1540, Hernando de Soto of Spain led the first group of Europeans to visit what is now Tennessee. De Soto and his men were looking for gold, which they did not find. They treated the Native Americans they met very badly, forcing them to work

for them and stealing from them. In addition, they carried diseases such as smallpox and measles. The Native Americans had no resistance to these new diseases, and many died. Another group of Spaniards looking for gold visited the area in 1566. After that, no Europeans explored Tennessee for more than one hundred years.

The next Europeans to come were the French and the English. In 1673, Father Jacques Marquette, a Catholic missionary, and fur trader Louis Joliet traveled the Mississippi River from Illinois to the Gulf of Mexico, claiming the land for France. More fur traders followed. The French traded with the Native Americans and built forts along the river. In the same year, Englishmen Gabriel Arthur and James Needham explored Tennessee from the east and began trading with the Cherokee.

The French and Indian War between France and England broke out in 1754 and lasted until 1763. Most Cherokee tribes fought for the British, while other tribes fought for the French. France lost the war, and had to give all its land in the Mississippi Valley to the British. What is now Tennessee became part of North Carolina, a British colony.

After the war, the British declared that no one was allowed to settle in land west of the Appalachian Mountains. They could not enforce this law. The chance to become rich hunting fur-bearing animals and selling their pelts and the opportunity to buy cheap land was too strong. Settlers began moving west over the mountains. One of the first overmountain communities was along the Watauga River far away from any government officials in North Carolina. In 1772, the community wrote its own constitution and elected officials who made and enforced the laws.

When the Revolutionary War (1775–1783) began, Tennessee was

Fort Loudoun was a British fort built in East Tennessee during the French and Indian War.

still part of North Carolina. The Cherokee were already angry about pioneers settling on their lands and hunting their game. Soon after the war started, the British encouraged the Cherokee to raid white settlements. The fort at Watauga was attacked, but the settlers held off the Cherokee. North Carolina and other southern states sent troops to reinforce the fort. These troops defeated the Cherokee and forced them to give up a large amount of their land. After that, although Tennessee sent volunteers to fight the British, no Revolutionary War battles were fought in the state.

In 1790, North Carolina gave the land south of the Ohio River that is now Tennessee to the federal government as payment for various debts. This land became the Southwest Territory. William Blount was appointed governor, but in reality, Native tribes controlled much of the land.

In 1791, the Southwest Territory had a population of 35,691. To become a state, the Territory needed a population of 60,000. Over the next five years, pioneers poured into the Territory. This caused conflict with Native tribes. On June 1, 1796, Tennessee was admitted to the Union

 ## The State of Franklin

After the Revolutionary War ended, leaders of three counties in East Tennessee wanted to break free from North Carolina and be recognized as an independent state. They wrote a constitution, elected John Sevier governor, and named the state Franklin. Franklin had many problems. For example, it had no currency. People were paid in animal pelts—"one thousand deerskins for the governor…four hundred and fifty otter skins for the governor's secretary, five hundred raccoon skins for each county clerk…" Franklin was never recognized by the federal government and fell apart after four years. However, when Tennessee was admitted as the sixteenth state, John Sevier became its first governor.

This cabin, built around 1822 by John Oliver and his wife Lucretia Frazier, was one of the first European settlements in Tennessee. It is located at Cade's Cove, where there had been a Cherokee village in the eighteenth and early nineteenth centuries. Today, the area is part of Great Smoky Mountains National Park.

as the sixteenth state. By then its population had more than doubled.

Britain and the United States went to war again from 1812 to 1814. Tennessee provided so many volunteers for this war that it earned the nickname, the Volunteer State. Once again, the British encouraged Native Americans, this time the Creek, to make war on pioneers in Tennessee and Alabama. Andrew Jackson led troops that defeated the Creek and forced them to give up most of their land. Jackson's troops then went on to defeat the British at the end of the war in the Battle of New Orleans.

After the War of 1812 ended, settlers continued to stream into Tennessee and other Southeastern states. These settlers wanted land for farming. This put them in conflict with the Native Americans who had been hunting and living on the land for hundreds of years. Andrew Jackson, president of the United States from 1829 to 1837, was forced to deal with this competition for land.

The first six presidents of the United States had been wealthy men from East Coast states. Andrew Jackson was the first frontier president. He was born into an immigrant

Andrew Jackson helped to found the state of Tennessee in 1796, was a hero of the War of 1812, and served as the seventh president of the United States from 1829 to 1837.

farming family in South Carolina, but lived his adult live in Tennessee. Jackson was a short-tempered, plain-spoken man who had become a national hero fighting Native Americans and the British. Jackson believed in equality of opportunity and that in America anyone who worked hard could become whatever he wanted to be, even president. However, his actions showed that he believed this to be true only for white Americans.

In order to provide new immigrants with land, the United States Congress passed, and Andrew Jackson signed, the Indian Removal Act. The Act forced the Cherokee, Choctaw, Creek, Chickasaw, Seminole tribes in the Southeast to leave their homelands and move west of the Mississippi River and into Indian Territory (now Oklahoma).

Removal began during Jackson's presidency and continued under Martin Van Buren, the president who followed Jackson. In 1838, soldiers rounded up 16,500 Cherokees and 2,000 slaves the Cherokees owned and forced them to walk 2,200 miles (3500 km) to Indian Territory. About

During the 1830s, the U.S. government implemented policies that removed Native Americans from their homes in Tennessee and other states, and forced them to move to the west.

4,000 died on the way. The route of their forced march is now the Trail of Tears National Historic Trail. A few Cherokee escaped the roundup and continued to live in the mountains of North Carolina, Tennessee, and Georgia. Today their descendants are recognized as the Eastern Band of the Cherokee Nation.

As the nation grew, slavery caused increased tension between North and South. Eventually the issue came to a head. South Carolina seceded from the Union on December 20, 1860 and the Civil War (1861–1865) began. Other states in the Deep South quickly followed. At first, Tennessee was reluctant to join these states. The small farmers in the mountains of East Tennessee did not depend on slave labor the way the cotton plantations along the Mississippi River did. East Tennessee wanted to stay in the Union while West Tennessee wanted to secede. After several votes, on June 8, 1861, Tennessee became the last of eleven states that joined the Confederate States of America (CSA).

About 115,000 Tennesseans fought for the CSA and another 30,000 for the Union. More Civil War battles were fought in Tennessee than in any other state except Virginia. Many of the battles were for control of the rivers and railroads that crisscrossed the state. One of the bloodiest was at Shiloh on April 2, 1862. By the time the Union won the battle, more than 23,000 Union and Confederate soldiers had been killed, injured, or captured.

When the Civil War ended in 1865, Tennessee was a damaged state. Many family farms had been destroyed when either army marched through the state *confiscating* horses, mules, and food or burning anything they thought might help the other side.

The period immediately following the Civil War is called Reconstruction. This was a period of great bitterness. African Americans were granted citizenship and equal protection under the law by the fourteenth amendment to the Constitution, but Tennesseans found ways to restrict their freedom. For example, the hate group, the Ku

The Battle of Shiloh was an important early clash in the Civil War. A large Union army commanded by Ulysses S. Grant was surprised by the Confederate Army on April 6, 1862. The Union forces were forced to retreat, but the Confederates did not press the attack. Union reinforcements arrived late that night, and Grant's army counterattacked the next day, driving the Confederates away.

The Battle of Franklin, fought November 30, 1864, was devastating defeat for the Confederate Army. John Bell Hood, the Confederate commander in the war's western theatre, insisted on attacking a fortified Union position at Franklin. Hood's Army of Tennessee suffered heavy casualties and was effectively destroyed as a fighting force.

Klux Klan (KKK), was founded in Pulaski, Tennessee in 1865. The KKK used violence to threaten and terrorize African Americans. Despite this, Tennessee became the first Confederate state to rejoin the Union on July 24, 1866. The state continued to enforce segregation until the 1960s.

Until the Civil War, Tennessee had been a rural state. After the war, although there were still many farms, cities such as Memphis, Chattanooga, and Nashville began to grow. Some northern manufacturers moved their factories to Tennessee to take advantage of cheap labor. Soon the state was producing cloth, iron, steel, and other manufactured goods.

World War I (1914–1918) gave a boost to manufacturing. Over 100,000 Tennesseans fought in the war. Many others found jobs in factories and on farms where they worked overtime to produce food and supplies for the troops.

Starting in 1929, the entire country was affected by the Great Depression. Factories and mines closed. As many as one-third of all men were unemployed. Families suffered, and there were few government programs to help them make ends

The Scopes Trial

In Tennessee in 1925, the Butler Act forbid the teaching of evolution or denying the Biblical account of the creation of man. The American Civil Liberties Union (ACLU) asked John Scopes, a substitute biology teacher, to intentionally teach the theory of evolution so that the law could be challenged. Scopes was defended by Clarence Darrow, an atheist, while William Jennings Bryan, three-time candidate for president of the United States and a fundamentalist Christian, was on the prosecution team. The jury found Scopes guilty and fined him $100. The case went to the Tennessee Supreme Court, which ruled the Butler Act constitutional. Teaching evolution remained illegal in the state until 1967 when the Butler Act was repealed.

meet. That changed when Franklin D. Roosevelt became president in 1933.

President Roosevelt promised a government-funded New Deal to put Americans back to work. In Tennessee, the New Deal created the Tennessee Valley Authority (TVA). This program made new jobs by building thirty-nine dams on Tennessee rivers to control flooding and produce electricity. The Works Progress Administration (WPA) put people to work building roads, airports, schools, and libraries. The Civilian Conservation Corps hired men to plant trees and develop parks.

These programs helped Tennesseans survive, but the Depression did not end until World War II (1941–1945) began and American farmers and factories worked overtime to support the war effort. Another way the war affected Tennessee was in the establishment of Oak Ridge, a town near Knoxville. This town was built specifically for scientists working to develop the atomic bomb. Today Oak Ridge National Laboratory focuses on energy, computing, and national security.

When soldiers returned from World War II, they returned to a segregated Tennessee. This began to change in the 1950s and 1960s. In 1954, the United States Supreme Court ruled that separate public schools for white and black children were unconstitutional. Although laws required integration of public schools and other public places, the change caused demonstrations, riots, and violence. On April 4, 1968, civil rights leader Martin Luther King Jr. was shot and killed while visiting Memphis to support striking African American workers.

Since the 1980s, Tennessee has gradually become a more prosperous and more industrial state. Foreign companies such as Toshiba and Sony have built manufacturing and distribution centers in Tennessee. This has brought new residents from many different backgrounds to the state. In addition, young Tennesseans are better educated than they were in the 1960s. Although the state lost jobs during the recession that began in

Construction of a hydro-electric dam on the French Broad River in east Tennessee, 1942. This dam was one of a series constructed by the Tennessee Valley Authority from the 1930s to the 1950s to bring electrical power to rural areas in Tennessee and neighboring states.

A meter has been installed on this rural home to measure the electricity delivered from the Tennessee Valley Authority's transmission line.

2008, by 2014 it had begun to recover as the national economy improved.

Government

Tennessee is governed from the capital, Nashville, under a constitution written during Reconstruction in 1870. The state constitution follows the organization of the U. S. Constitution with three branches of state government: executive, legisla-tive, and judicial. Like the U.S. Constitution, the Tennessee constitution contains a bill of rights for the citizens of the state.

The executive branch of government consists of the governor, lieu-tenant governor, secretary of state, treasurer, *comptroller* of the treasury, and the heads of twenty-one depart-ments such as education, health, and agriculture. These department heads

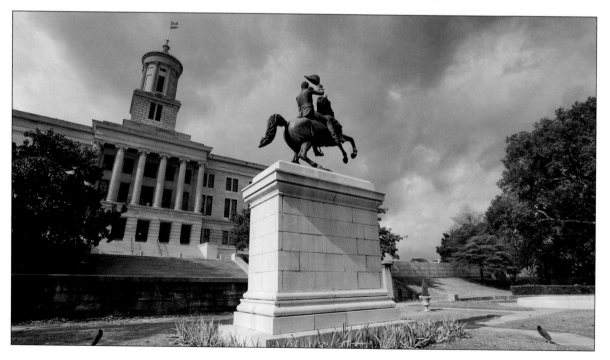

A statue of Andrew Jackson stands outside the Tennessee State Capitol building in Nashville.

are appointed by the governor. The governor also prepares the state budget and approves or vetoes bills passed by the legislature.

The governor is elected in a statewide election every four years. A candidate for governor must be an American citizen at least thirty years old who has lived in Tennessee for seven or more years. Governors can serve only two terms in a row. The speaker (head) of the state senate serves as the lieutenant governor and takes over if the governor dies. The secretary of state, treasurer, and comptroller are elected by the legislature instead of being elected by the public.

The legislature, called the General Assembly, is responsible for writing and passing bills. It has two houses. The state House of Representatives has ninety-nine members who serve two-year terms. The state Senate has thirty-three members who serve four-year terms. Candidates for either house must be American citizens, have lived in Tennessee for at least three years, and be at least twenty-one years old.

Lamar Alexander served as governor of Tennessee from 1979 to 1987, and has represented the state in the U.S. Senate since 2003.

The judicial branch is headed by the state Supreme Court. The court has five elected judges who serve eight-year terms. The judges elect one member to be chief justice. They also elect the attorney general, who is the head law enforcement officer of the state. Under the Supreme Court are the Court of Appeals, which hears appeals of civil cases such as contract disputes, and the Court of Criminal Appeals, which deals with appeals of criminal trials. Below these are specialized courts that hear criminal cases or various types of civil and family disputes.

Tennessee sends two Senators and nine Representatives to Washington to represent the state in Congress. This gives Tennessee eleven electoral votes in presidential elections.

The Economy

The first Europeans to enter Tennessee found fur-bearing animals such as otter, mink, and raccoon. Many early East Tennesseans made their living hunting and selling the skins of these animals. Others planted crops and raised chickens and hogs to feed their families or raised tobacco as a cash crop. The invention of the cotton gin, which removed seeds from cotton fibers, made it profitable to grow cotton in the land along the Mississippi River in West Tennessee. Tennessee was mainly an agricultural state until the mid-1930s. Today agriculture is less important to the state's economy. Soybeans are the most valuable crop. Farmers also raise wheat, tobacco, cotton, nursery plants, beef cattle, and chickens on about 80,000 farms.

Although the Depression of the 1930s caused great hardship, it also changed Tennessee in a way that made it more attractive to manufacturers. The Tennessee Valley Authority (TVA) was part of President Franklin Roosevelt's New Deal program

Tennessee has become a major center for automobile manufacturing. In addition to this Volkswagen plant in Chattanooga, Nissan and General Motors also operate manufacturing facilities in the state. There are also about 1,000 smaller auto-related businesses in Tennessee, providing more than 115,000 jobs.

designed to put people who had lost their jobs back to work. The TVA built dams that created waterpower that could be turned into electricity. The Rural Electrification Administration, another New Deal program, strung miles of power lines to bring electricity to areas that previously had none. Abundant electricity, low labor costs, and access to rivers and railroads to transport goods encouraged manufacturers to build factories in Tennessee.

Norris Dam in east Tennessee is one of many power-generating facilites operated by the Tennessee Valley Authority. Established by Congress in 1933, TVA today is the nation's largest public power provider. It provides electricity to more than 9 million people, serving most of Tennessee as well as parts of Alabama, Georgia, Kentucky, Mississippi, North Carolina, and Virginia.

Today Tennessee factories process raw materials such as cotton into cloth and agricultural products such as wheat and corn into foods like bread and cereal. Cars roll off the assembly line at several plants in the state, while other factories produce parts for those cars, chemicals, paint, and rubber products. Manufacturing makes up about 12 percent of Tennessee's economy. Mining of coal, limestone, and zinc make up about another 3 percent.

As in most of the United States, today the service industry is the largest part of Tennessee's economy. Service jobs are jobs in areas such as education, health care, tourism, and entertainment where no physical products are made. The music industry is especially important to the state's economy. Nashville is the capital of country music. In addition to many jobs related to making and selling music, Nashville attracts thousands of tourists every year who come to hear country music stars perform. Other tourists come to hike and camp in state parks and Great Smoky Mountain National Park or to visit Civil War battlefields such as Shiloh. Tennessee's geographic and cultural diversity give the state a well-balanced economy.

The People

In the census of 1800, Tennessee had a population of 105,602, of which 13,584 (12.8 percent) were slaves. Native Americans were not counted as a separate group. By 2013, the population had grown to almost 6.5 million. About one-third of the population lives in rural areas. The rest live in cities and towns.

In 2013, about 4.5 percent of the state's residents had been born in a foreign country, and 6.6 percent spoke a language other than English at home. These numbers are much lower than the national average. In the nation as a whole, 12.9 percent of individuals were not born in the United States, and 20.5 percent do not speak English at home.

In 2013, 79.4 percent of the population self-identified as white. This is higher than the national average of 62.6 percent. On the other hand, only

Famous People from Tennessee

When the Cherokee Sequoyah (c1765–1836) saw Europeans communicating in writing, he understood what a powerful tool written language was. Sequoyah invented a system of written syllables that could be used to represent the spoken language of the Cherokee. This helped preserve many Cherokee stories and customs for future generations.

Davy Crockett (1786–1836) was born in East Tennessee. He joined the Army, fought against the Creeks and the Seminoles, and was elected to the U.S. Congress. Later he moved to Texas and died defending the Alamo. Today he represents the rough and ready frontiersman to many Americans.

Davy Crockett

Three presidents lived in Tennessee at the time they were elected, although none were born in the state. Andrew Jackson (1767–1845), the seventh president, was the first president to come from west of the Appalachian Mountains. James K. Polk (1795–1849), the eleventh president, favored expansion of the United States westward to the Pacific Ocean. Andrew Johnson (1808–1875) was a senator from Tennessee. When his state joined the Confederacy, Johnson stayed in the United States Senate. He became Abraham Lincoln's vice president and took over after Lincoln was killed. He had the difficult job of overseeing Reconstruction and the return of southern states to the Union.

A more recent politician, Al Gore (b. 1948) served as a representative and then a senator in the U.S. Congress. He was vice president under Bill Clinton and ran for president in 2000, but lost in a disputed election. Since then, he has worked to educate people about environmental issues, particularly climate change.

Many musicians were either born in Tennessee or started their careers there. These include Carl Perkins (1932–1998), Aretha Franklin (b. 1942), Dolly Parton (b. 1946), and Miley Cyrus (b. 1992). Rock legends B.B. King (b. 1925) and Elvis Presley (1935–1977) started their careers in Memphis, while pop star Taylor Swift (b. 1989) began hers in Nashville.

The University of Tennessee in Knoxville, founded in 1794, is one of the oldest universities in the United States. More than 20,000 undergraduate students are enrolled there.

about 5 percent self-identified as Hispanic or Latino, a much lower percentage than in the nation as a whole, where 17 percent of the population is Hispanic/Latino. Blacks or African Americans made up 17 percent of the population. The number of African Americans living in the state has been increasing since1990. Asians made up only 1.6 percent of Tennessee's residents, while a tiny 0.4 percent of Tennesseans were Native Americans. All other groups combined, including those who identified with two or more races, totaled less than 2 percent.

A higher percentage of Tennesseans (56 percent) actively practice a religion than people in the nation as a whole (48 percent). Of people who are religious, the vast majority (82 percent) are Christian. Protestants make up 70 percent of these Christians. More than half of these Protestant Christians belong to Baptist churches. Roman Catholics make up about 6 percent of churchgoers. Less than 3 percent of the population practices another religion such as Islam, Judaism, or Hinduism.

Young people in Tennessee graduate from high school and earn four-year college degrees at a slightly lower rate than the national average.

People in Tennessee earn less money than the national average income. Between 2008 and 2012, the median household income in Tennessee was $44,140, about $9,000 less than the national average. About 17 percent of residents have incomes that fall below the poverty level. However, a slightly higher percentage of Tennesseans own their home than the national average.

The Grand Ole Opry is a landmark in Nashville that draws country music fans from around the world.

(Left) The neon signs of famous blues clubs line Beale Street in Memphis. Beale Street is a major tourist attraction and a place for blues festivals and concerts. (Bottom) View of the Memphis skyline from the Mississippi River with a marina in the foreground.

Major Cities

Memphis, located on the Mississippi River in the southwest corner of Tennessee, is the largest city in the state. Memphis International Airport is the second busiest cargo airport in the world thanks to FedEx, the express package service, whose head-quarters are in the city. Music and Memphis have always gone together. Musical styles originating in the city include the Memphis blues, Memphis soul, rock 'n roll, and crunk, a form of southern hip hop. Beale Street, the home of the blues, is a national historic landmark, and thousands of

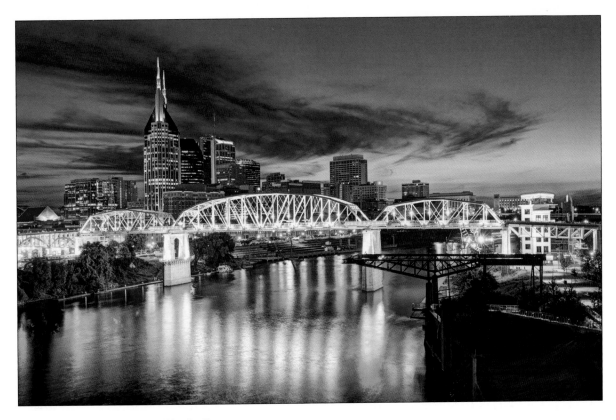

The skyline of downtown Nashville.

Each year, more than 600,000 people visit Graceland, the Memphis mansion of Elvis Presley. Today, the home is operated as a museum, and is on the National Register of Historic Places.

tourists come to visit Graceland, the home of Elvis Presley.

Nashville is not only the state capital, it is the capital of country music. Located on the Cumberland River in the central part of the state, Nashville is home to many major record labels, Gibson Guitar, and the Grand Ole Opry. The Opry has been broadcasting a radio hour of country music, bluegrass, and skits since 1925. Nashville is also home to several universities, including Vanderbilt, Tennessee State, Fisk, and Meharry Medical College. The city has two professional sports teams, the Tennessee Titans of the National Football League and the National Hockey League Nashville Predators.

In the Appalachian region of East Tennessee, *Knoxville* is the site of the main campus of the University of Tennessee, one of the city's largest employers. Knoxville is also home to the Women's Basketball Hall of Fame and minor league soccer, ice hockey, and baseball teams. Almost every month Knoxville celebrates with a festival ranging from the International

Biscuit Festival to Kuumba, a festival of African heritage, to the Rossini festival celebrating dance and opera.

Interesting smaller towns in Tennessee include *Gatlinburg*, the gateway to Great Smoky Mountain National Park; *Bristol*, home of Bristol Motor Speedway; and *Pigeon Forge*, where families can enjoy Dollywood amusement park.

Further Reading

Bobrick, Benson. *The Battle of Nashville: General George H. Thomas & the Most Decisive Battle of the Civil War.* New York: Knopf Books for Young Readers, 2010.

Herman, Gail. *Who Was Davy Crockett?* New York: Grosset & Dunlap, 2013.

Hollar, Sherman, ed. *Andrew Jackson.* New York: Britannica Educational Pub. in association with Rosen Educational Services, 2013.

Kallen, Stuart A. *The History of Country Music.* Detroit: Lucent Books, 2012.

Luna, Kristin. *Tennessee Curiosities: Quirky Characters, Roadside Oddities & Other Offbeat Stuff.* Guilford, Conn.: Globe Pequot Press, 2011.

Petreycik, Rick. *It's My State! Tennessee.* New York: Cavendish Square, 2014.

 # Text-Dependent Questions

1. What are the major land regions in Tennessee?
2. What was the Indian Removal Act?
3. What were some of the programs in Franklin Roosevelt's New Deal?

Internet Resources

http://www.civilwar.org

The Civil War Trust ia a non-profit organization devoted to preserving Civil War battlefields. The website contains general information about the war and specific information about individual battles.

http://www.tn.gov

The official website of the State of Tennessee provides up-to-date information about government services, the economy and breaking news about the state.

http://www.teachtnhistory.org

Resources for students and teachers with links to primary sources can be found at Teach Tennessee History.

http://www.tnhistoryforkids.org

Tennessee History for Kids provides educational booklets and videos organized by grade level, including links to primary sources

http://www.tnvacation.com

The official tourism site for the state of Tennessee is organized by region and attractions.

 **Research Project**

Imagine you are living in Tennessee in 1939. Investigate the work of the Tennessee Valley Authority and the Rural Electrification Administration during the Great Depression. Write a few paragraphs about how your life is different in 1939 from the way it was ten years earlier in 1929 because of these organizations.

Index

Numbers in **bold italics** refer to captions.

Series Glossary of Key Terms

bicameral—having two legislative chambers (for example, a senate and a house of representatives).

cede—to yield or give up land, usually through a treaty or other formal agreement.

census—an official population count.

constitution—a written document that embodies the rules of a government.

delegation—a group of persons chosen to represent others.

elevation—height above sea level.

legislature—a lawmaking body.

precipitation—rain and snow.

term limit—a legal restriction on how many consecutive terms an office holder may serve.